# PERIPETEIA

## LISA RHODES-RYABCHICH

Dedication :

To my father who told me try to write something funny, which probably saved my life and to my most precious daughter, Kyla Jolie Ryabchich you are the one that is joyful and always the sunshine in my life, even on the most darkest days; I know you will be there for me. You are so kind; I really love you! And I know you will overcome the challenges of this life. I wish you miracles!

Finally, to single mothers everywhere, enjoy your hour of truth; you have been resurrected! Namaste.

# Contents

# THE BEST METAPHOR ABOUT DEATH JOKE

I'd like to dedicate this, to all the newly departed,
absent, non-child supporting fathers, now all together,


and listen to their stories, and trials of parenting,
and place them on a cd, and blast them through the speakers,


to the other world, and shame the fathers, still unsure,
of what it is, to be above a heartless seer, and rattle


their cages, with bubblegum, and teddy bears, and jingling
bells, and birthday cakes, and candles. Mother's, put the stamp


of bewilderment, and impossibility in your backpack,
and carry it to the top of Mount Everest, and dangle the metaphor,


like a moth, flitting against the light, flickering the worms away,
from the newly departed dead, waiting to break the barrier


of laughter, to fill the universe with gleeful diapers, containing
golden nuggets. Oh, so many blossoms will bloom, straight

to the root of happiness, planted here on Earth, even if the dad's
names are ghostly flashing all over billboards, and auto mechanic shops,


and TV commercials, and songs. Oh, so many shit-filled songs…
of how they shouldn't have had to die, and *why didn't I get
buried*


*this way, or that way, even though I was too cheap to buy*
a life insurance policy, or make a good grief will or rumple my ass,


to pay my health bills, or even learn how to make love.

# THE ORNITHOLOGIST IN THE AIRPORT AFTER URINATING HIS LAST VODKA TONIC

There is a sprig, of cool birch wood
Here, beneath the big Air China
Sign


And it looks like I am back
In the forest of Taipei.
I have a belt, made
From the bark, of a cinnamon tree—
Golden brown, burnt, like an Orangutans fur.


Did you know, this lounge,
Once had Kris Kristofferson, playing
Songs, about the loss of his first love? —
Blasting from his tongue,
After a night of binge drinking,
Coming back from L.A.
I could have hugged him, all night.


My legs are swaying and scissoring,
From toiling like a food processor.
The arrangement of handmade stars,
As the lights are flickering,
To the music, is like the songs,
Of the most beautiful Daurian Redstart, breathing life.

# AFTER WATCHING "THE PRICE IS RIGHT"

A male contestant added $1.00 to the heavy homemaker's bid.
The prize package was an assortment of hiking gear, definitely


Not the prize she was expecting anyway. What do you know—
In a second, he is the winner! He quickly bounds onto stage,


Grin plastered from cheek to cheek. He exclaims, "I've just
Hiked some of those dangerous trails!" With a spin of the magic


Wheel, he is smoodged with a trip to *Patagonia,* land of serenity
And hiking trails infinitesimal. Hike till the island makes you dizzy.


No boredom here, lots of fish, hiking, relaxation, and fine dining.
You won't have to worry about noise. No clowns to bother you.


No movies to titillate your senses. No air pollution to escape,
Just fresh air and the quiet of rattlesnakes, lizards and birds


Serenading you to sleep. Lots of glaciers to keep your hot flashes
humming. A small chance of a snowstorm. No worries, the
kitchen is stocked

With fresh fish galore, a variety of vegetables and music,
Lots of soft meditating music. No disco lights to cause double vision,


Or to feign madness, when your wife wants a rum coke,
And she's back from rehab, only two weeks. Life here seems


Too serene, to cause any stir, even when the leaves rustle,
And a Peeping Tom peers in, from the miniature window outside


Your room. No alarms go off— no worries. The phone isn't connected
Yet. There are no local Police, just rangers with *Uzi's,* to frighten away,


Any rehabilitated alcoholic, who left her wallet, back on flight 777,
Destined to provide her with a preview, of the heavenly island,


With her husband's new Toyota L, equipped with automatic transmission.
Life could be worse— her husband could have won a Jaguar, with a trip


To Africa, to romp with the poachers, roaming the wild, deter-
mined to skin
As many pellets of fur, to sell to a westerner for trophies, to
garnish their walls,


And to stimulate conversations with their *conservationist*
wealthy guests,
About creating ways for how they can contribute, anonymously,

To *Save The Wildlife Fund*, which will earn them a million
*Karma points*,
In the paradise of their choice. This seems to her better, than
listening to the MC,


On *The Price Is Right,* who says repeatedly in manic speech, faster
Then you can process Abracadabra, "You're having quite a day,


Quite a day, how about that folks!" in his Cleveland twang,
After the lilting ring of the winning bid, jerks her better, than the
*Rehab Director.*

# RENDEZVOUS AT THE AZALEA GARDEN RESTAURANT

"You have the shape
Of a fine manicured lawn:
Neat and clean.
Let me take your hand—


you just won the award
for the most photogenic,
handsome man with the best musky aroma!
Do you travel a lot?"


"No, my wife is waiting for me—
At the Azalea Garden Restaurant
A mile away, I gotta go. See ya."


"This is the most sensual dining &
Cuisine arrangement. Look honey
At the view. We made it—


Overlooking the sunset."
From a corner booth the woman hides
& watches under antique tinted

Pince Nez silver tone eyeglasses.
"Damn that arrogant slimy ring-necked snake!"
She looks just like me except


Her hair is red and her clothes
Are shabby. My neighbor's dog
Wears better clothes and I


Don't have the time to own
A dog; I have no patience
For such problems—the urinating


On the floor—the endless hours
Of training them to not eat my shoes;
The doggy hair enmeshed in my cereal bowl.


And the potential lawsuits after it bit someone.
I have better things to do with my time!
Life is short; I could be traveling the world—


Listening to beautiful music, meeting with
Scholars and peacemakers and  artists.
Oh, such is the soul that touches me


When I least expect it. Life with its red,
Red Carpets plastered all over walls
Stretched out from New York

To San Francisco is only better
Than roses on Valentine's Day
Or my lover's tongue stuck in


My ear and I'm feeling nothing
But disgust, no zing of cinnamon
Or a twang of mango or papaya


To sweeten things up—
No Taj Mahal; no Nirvana
From the sun splitting open my brain.

# A SWEET TOOTH MEMORY

When I was five years-old, my drop-dead, handsome Papa with
the charisma of Clark Gable, stopped his shiny, blue 4-door Buick

Skylark sedan, on Amsterdam—the west side of New York City—
the newest epicenter of bustling opportunity & raw creativity

where he did business. I remember a sweet Greek shopkeeper behind a
counter pleasantly charmed by little me. She gave me a triple decker

strawberry ice-cream cone. It tasted like heaven. My papa then
was a Borden's ice cream salesman, and she owned a mom &
pop ice cream parlor.

She smiled so kindly like an angelic angel. It was great being Papa's
little girl— just being lucky and living in New York City.

Years later, when I was prepping for boarding school,
I worked in his Real Estate office. In the summer morning,
we would eat cinnamon buns, and drink sweet coffee

from Dennis' coffee shop. I later sat at his back desk where a
ceramic heart that I had made in kindergarten shouted, "I Love
You Papa" as I read *The New York Times*.


When I was bored, I would rifle in his desk drawer and sort
through junk: Jacks, stickers, baseball cards and stale, pink bubble
gum left from an employee's kid who had sat there too.


And next door was a handbag store, called Can Can
that sold cool, colorful duffel and handbags with flair to make you dance.


Sadly, they eventually went out of business. Then, years later
Denny, the owner of the coffee shop died of cancer. And the best
memory remaining, is of the poster


plastered in Papa's storefront window of a straggly, grey-haired,
withered, American Indian woman, smoking a fat, brown, smelly
Cuban cigar with the caption: "Aren't I glamorous?"

# WHAT I THINK OF THE BABYSITTERS WHO TELL ME THEY WONT' BABYSIT MY DISABLED CHILD

1. Don't tell me, you have no capacity, to change a child's pull-up.

2. Don't tell me, you forgot to put her on the toilet, because you forgot, she ever urinated like *a real person.*

3. Don't tell me, you could *never learn* how to play, with a cortically blind child, who smiles and laughs, after you tell her, *"you're beautiful."*

4. Don't tell me, you *don't know* what it feels like, to want to be accepted, and be like all the other kids, in your neighborhood.

5. Don't tell me, you never wanted to make a difference, in the life of a cerebral palsied child and help then feel *normal.*

6. Don't tell me, you don't feel the desire to *give back* to your community.

7. Don't tell me, you never *once* thought, you could be me: a single mother with a disabled child whom you love to death.

8.    Don't tell me, my life is *contagious,* and you might catch
      hell, when you're having kids, if you babysat mine.


9.    Don't tell me, that people like me, deserve to be discriminated
      against, and that my life, and my child's life, *don't matter*.


10.   Don't tell me, I'm a *bad parent,* for wanting to go to work,
      or to go out for a few hours *alone,* to refresh my mind, and
      lighten up my life.


11.   Don't tell me, what you think about me, *inadvertently,* with
      your poem directed at your lover, where you tear apart their
      looks, and actlike
      I'm supposed to feel frightened, because maybe I could fit
      the bill too, or be the *stand-in* for them, whenever you felt
      like it.


12.   Or is it this *anti-feminist* thing, where all females are the
      enemy, and I should have known that I gotmine?


13.   I never knew that a person, could be such a catty bum, and
      *Kruk-you so and so* and never have anything happen, to
      their perfect baby bag of dreams!


14.   I know you want to believe, that your life is *perfect,* and I'm
      supposed to know that, by the way you lie, and say you're
      always *busy,* when I ask you to  babysit.

15.     Why act like you're such a *superior A hole,* with so much
        education and experience, when you can't even *assist* lifting,
        a *100-pound* bag of salt,
        or save anybody from *choking,* or perform CPR, or wash a
        kid's face
        or hands, or check their pull-up bag, or help them play with
        their dolls,
        or blow bubbles, or give a kid a squishy toy, or laugh,
        *or help* a kid feel *OK*, or even *happy.*

# YOU WILL NEVER BELIEVE THIS

We're waiting in my 2013, needs a bath car, to leave the parking
garage,
after visiting the hospital, to return EEG equipment, and suddenly


this life force— this aesthetic—this electricity— this enlightened
spell—
this *vision* of my daughter, appears to me, of her coming out of her


body, and floating over the head, of a *dumb, gumby girl*, in love,
with
her boyfriend, to not be mourned—due to unconsciousness, blissful
love—


stoned— unable to see straight, oh to be blinded by love, to walk
into a car
enamored, but my daughter miraculously perceiving, my fright,
knowing


what will happen, had removed herself from her epileptic, ex-
hausted
in-a-trance body, then possessed the body of the *dumb, gumby
girl*, as I watched


in disbelief, as she loomed over her head, and I caught the boyfriend looking at my astonished face, before he pushed his girlfriend back

onto the curb, so she doesn't get smashed by a car. A true death
or injury, surely would have occurred. Miracle…for everyone.

God *forbid* something should happen to my daughter,
sitting in the back seat, already *zoned-out* in a trance…

She has used her *powers,* to heal and save, *a total stranger.*
I hope they appreciate her *heroism,* in helping them survive, and
pass it on!

# FALLING IN LOVE AFTER A DIAGNOSIS OF BIPOLAR DISORDER

A News article said: a figure skating star


Debbie Thomas just announced in 2015 that she had to close
her medical practice because:

1.  Life savings gone.

2.  Lost custody of her teenage son, after suffering two divorces.
    (Red flag goes up here! Can't a person fail at the institution
    of marriage, and still be a good mom?)


As a result:

1.  She is now living, in a bedbug-infested trailer, with her
    alcoholic
    fiancée and his two sons.


2.  Motivational coach, Iyania Vanzant, and star of the reality
    TV show,
    *Fix My Life* promises to help her turn her life around.

Her short program in 1987 was:

    "Something in my house," by Dead or Alive,

1. Hey, Debbie, wake up. This song seems to be your current situation.

2. With the bedbugs crawling around your trailer, it's enough to make anyone crazy.

3. Just think your breakfast bowl has red creatures staring back at you, so, you're definitely not *dead or alive,* at least not mentally.

4. Turn on the lights; take some lithium—enough to get your self-respect back, because living with someone, who is sick, and cohabitating
with them, can be a DISASTER.

5. If you had to auction your bronze medal off, for *two million dollars*, it's possible
*someone* would buy it.

6. You can get *somebody* better, then that *stone-faced* fiancée. You're better than this!

7. Alcoholism can be managed, and so can Bipolar Disorder.

8. Lithium isn't a *life sentence*. It adds life to your brain cells. If you can live

your life in a fulfilling way, or if you're *done* with the lithium, try SAM-e, because it works too!

9.  Get on the bandwagon! Enough of the guilt trip. Repair your relationship with your son.
    He may forgive you!

10. Remember, mental illness can be managed.

11. Debbie give yourself a *gold medal* for rehabilitation!

# Peripeteia

Is changing lanes, away from the *weary trucker,* trying
To squeeze into your LANE


Or the *lone, racist trucker,* suddenly chasing you
Down the Vermont highway, at 100 miles per


Hour, and your wheelchair enabled daughter, is
There in the backseat, playing obliviously, happy with


Her beautiful dimples, sitting next to her new
Au Pair, from Namibia, who is fully trained,


In the complexities, of how to raise
A disabled child. After telling me, about her two previous stints


With families, with *Special Needs* kids, and getting
*Shit* on her head, as one child's uncontrollable bowels,


Exploded all over the place…
She tells me in a serious tone, "Your kid really isn't that bad."

Interestingly enough, her old host mom, was also her
Community counselor, and used a series of scare tactics


To keep her in her place. *No private entrance to bathe, just
take a trek through the kitchen, to find your shower!*


*No worries when the camel cries at night,
Just, put in your earplugs… Better this
way.*


*Nobody will know; no police report… just died in her sleep.*

# WHY I SHOULDN'T WORRY SO MUCH

I don't think, I'm getting younger.
I'm getting *blacker:* legs darkened
By age, a thigh, burned from spilling a
Scalding teacup from the microwave
Without a glove, that may not have fit
Wise fingers, like wheat bread
Toasted with a greasy layer of,
*Gee I Can't Believe It's Not Butter*, and
Veins plumped from *Lipitor,* now easy
To pry off the bone.


If your artery & veins are interconnected
By an *arteriovenous fistula,*
You may have an arm of valleys
And slopes, bulging prominently
From sloppy dialysis technicians,
Poking you, numerous times.


If your veins say, *drink from me,*
Your life will never run out.
Easy access is success every day
Of the week, even on holidays,
When nobody is working in the hospital,
And when you're newly graduated
Medical interns, are looking to make it
Out the door, to the after parties.

Hopefully, not after getting you
To your *afterlife.*


Being fat, around the tummy,
Means, you might be a runner up
For type II diabetes.
Being lazy, and never exercising
Is like waiting for a heart-*atta*ck,
To come *waltzing,* onto your plane,
Into your life, onto your job,
Into your condo, into your mind.
But now that I'm in shape, I can finally unwind.

# WHAT THE VAGINA MONOLOGUES INSPIRED

I'm sitting & thinking, with my daughter
at a Starbucks, & happy about my new


found freedom, to enjoy life.
The lyric from the song, "Jet Airliner" *Don't want*


*To get caught up in any of that funky shit in the city,*
*O big ol' Jet airliner…* kept ringing in


my ears & titillating my brain, so immediately
I transcended back, into a Girl Scout,


tapping out the music, to 1960s
groove. The sun was lit from orange pop,


Janis Joplin, yellow submarines,
sunflowers, Charlie Brown & daisies…


Orangeburg NY: The suburbs, where posters were flaming
of *copper tone skin,* boasting from a drugstore window,

& Sun In, promising to make my brown hair orange streaks, &
Tube Tops to make me the woman of my dreams: "NOW"


free to be sexy & cool. Lip-gloss came in little pots
of sugary grape frost, to dazzle my taste buds, & flash my pretty lips


like the models, in *Teen Magazine,* who knew who was dating who, in
*The Partridge Family*, & David Cassidy's fan club spilled gossip


about Shirley Jones, & oh those Barbies, lots of pretty Barbies &
Kiddles were the rage. Hot pants adorned every ass & hip.


*What hot pants, shall I wear today? Gotta go buy, lots of hot pants—*
*the shorter the better, & more colorful!*


Years later, after graduating from college, my mother scolded me,
after I donned, *flaming chili pepper red hot pants—*


"Always wear a rubber! A rubber!" as her black cane waved
vehemently.


 Once, I tried one of those female rubbers, that spread


out like a vast bottle seal. It wasn't so bad! My boyfriend
wasn't so keen, on wearing a rubber, but they were giving them away

for *free,* at the college where *The Vagina Monologues*
was performed. I thought, *I should at least have one in my
pocketbook,*

just in case, & because I am cool & hip, doing my thing,
no boyfriend can leave his germs on me!

# HOW TO GET EVEN WITH A SKINNY & SHORT SALES JERK

The Girl at the TD Bank Drive up
Was the same Girl who lied


At Lord &Taylor and said *you packed things*
*She didn't ring*—after she refused
To bag your employee purchase.


Instead of her saying—
"I deliberately set you up
By not ringing all those items,
Because I was jealous of those pretty suits
You were buying."


"So, when you left, the alarm
Went off and security
Took you away."


What if the reverse could be done?
And she walked away *red handed?*


Would the undercover police enter
From the parking lot?

Handcuff her to a tree?
Throw Gefilte fish down


Her shirt; nail her fingers to sticky paper?
Write *kruk you* on her face?


Beat her with a bamboo stick?
Make her play *Chinese checkers*


All night long? Put her teeth in
A denture cup? Pop her blackheads


With a screwdriver? Draw circles over
Her naked body? Scribble red paint on
her cheeks?


Invite all the birds to Come *shit* on her
head and post


A *Do Not Enter* sign on her forehead.

# On the heated night of Broadway

At 43<sup>rd</sup> street,
In skinny black pants—
Fly stuck
Like an old, broken
Accordion had playing out
Its last chord
Of music—and
Standing, was a homeless
Man dancing, to
James Brown music
With a cardboard sign
Gleaming white light
Under the hot sun:
*I only Dance If You Pay*.
He did a slick, shimmy
Stride on a wooden board,
Waxed like smooth velvet,
And moved his arms,
And pointy-booted feet
In a robotic trance—
Then ceased to perform,
Like a toy with worn
Down batteries, stuffed
In the back of its body,
Until his head, nodded
Slowly, slowly, slowly…
Before a coin was dropped
In his tin can, making

His head spin, to pick
Up the beat, doing
A slick, shimmy stride.

# A COUPLE DIES WHILE HAVING HOT TUB SEX
# AT THEIR DAUGHTER'S WEDDING

Oh, thank you God for meeting us here. We
needed to see you. We needed to  know,


You existed, in such a great *kind* way.
Knowing makes us wish, everyone on earth


Would just be *Green eggs & ham happy.*
No worries, no *alligator tears*, just enjoy!


And God, did it really have to happen this way?
I wish we could have planned a few things first,


Like Mozart music, for everyone to listen to at our funerals, so no
fears.
I want to say, we had a swell life … No


Anxieties. *I made love* most star struck weekends.
I enjoyed my warm summers, tending to my backyard,

Watering the Zinnias, and trying to grow thriving sunflowers,
taller than those, in the fields of Portugal.


I don't want to be remembered, as dying so tragically.
Oh, I hope they aren't *obsessed* silly about us!


Just let them hear our voices, in the bells of the distant *Cathedral,*
& in the clink of their frosted wine glasses, glimmering


In the sunlight—tipping off their *Vanity Fair* mirrors. Let them
know, our devoted love
              like the Himalayas, that shout out to
them, *Nirvana, Nirvana…*

# HOW GOD ESCAPED THE PENALTY OF BEING BARTERED AT STARBUCKS

Today it's Thursday, in the suburbs
of New York, and I'm in a Starbucks
and there is a guy, with orange tint,
in his hair, and gullible eyes and cheeks of
a sheep, and the holy bible


is sitting on the table, as barter
for your God, and is there a God like this—
whose God is the *holiest* God, and where
the orange star glitters atop the grain,
packaged on the desert, for the orphans,


and refuges, homeless across the Saharan
countries, waiting like pumpkins, or bags
full of hay, and gunnysacks are what's
left, after the food is distributed—
for clothes, and fabric for women, to make


handbags and pillows to sell to westerners,
who come for a glimpse, at this final stop
for all those to take what they can buy, and
dump the rest, for their money
can't buy peace or dreams, but *sweet hope*

that erases the confines of religion,
and which sets free, the voices for change,
so that there won't be a nuclear explosion,
and you know, they are sitting
at a handicapped accessible table,
and the handicapped sign is perched


at the edge of the table, and above it, is
a photo of 10s of 100's, of packed gunnysacks
lined up, and in the middle of the gunnysacks
is the shape of a big heart, and rays of light gleamed
down, reflecting a shadow of a big bird, waiting to
take off on a beautiful, relaxing vacation.

# SELF-PORTRAIT AS I'LL FIGHT UNTIL THE END

Praying each time, I leave my house—
    an apartment, to get the mail & go outside for a bike
ride, with my multiply handicapped daughter or
    to meet my disabled sister in the lobby


for a package pickup, knowing that it may be the day, *she's*
    *depressed and doesn't want to wear a mask*
or has no fear of germs on the door handles, going into and
    out of my building lobby or doesn't fear


the germs of people in the supermarket or the nursing home
    she visits or the air she breathes in or doesn't
keep a 6 feet distance because *they* are wearing a mask
    and she forgets to wash her hands after coughing or


spray the toilet after using it or diet when she's
    at least fifty pounds overweight.
I'm trying my damndest to remove the tire from my waist
    and my daughters. No extra servings of food,


just a cringe if I eat, and don't feel good about it.
    I'm a sensitive psychic, listening

to the footsteps of ghosts parading in my living room,
    hung up like mildew if I don't remember them correctly.


Yes, the dead speak to me. I'm not kidding!
    *Don't use the exclamation point!*
I remember a writing teacher telling me.

    But I use it anyway, the same way


I say what I feel when I think you're not listening.
    And the lives of those around you hang in the balance.
Yes, I'm going to fight with you!

# SELF PORTRAIT AS A PIECE OF TOFU AND AVOCADO

I am sitting on the second refrigerator shelf,
covered by clear, plastic wrap and
swimming in a tub, of chalky colored water.


I am extra hard, edible and nutritious. I am
made from the soybean. I am full of estrogen.
I may prevent Cancer or hot flashes.


I am an avocado, not yet ripe, light green and fatty inside,
under my thick, dark, green skin. I may increase,
your good cholesterol, if you use me in small portions.


I combine well with American cheese and plum tomatoes.
I would love to be made into a fabulous wedding cake,
with rose pink frosting. I would like to be so sweet that


even on a day when food was scarce, I still tasted great!
My biggest fear is that I will spoil, before being enjoyed
by some hungry, health-conscious person. I don't want to

smell foul, then become slimy and grossly gooey to touch.
I don't want to turn yellow then poison ... I need to relax, soaking
in some rich water after lathering on sunblock


to protect my sensitive skin. I have the mind of a cave woman,
useful, and creative. I am as precious as the full moon, enhancing
the appetites of little children. I was born from a big seed, so
beautiful, like the azure blue eggs of the blue bird.

# WHAT SHOULD HAPPEN TO MY ENEMIES

What unlucky human has a defect in their *Jeep  Cherokee,*
and it jumps out of gear and backs up, and pins a victim against
the bars of a gate and kills them? Why did this happen, to actor
Anton Yelchin, from the movie, *Star Trek?* This should happen to
my enemies—to have *their* automobile, kill them, accidentally.
No police report.
No blame. A simple annihilation.
No joke went sour.
No feelings out of control.
No alibi. No intent. No jury.
No verdict. No psychological
disorder. No lack of gun
control laws were to fault.
No tears for the perpetrators
Family. No lifetime of punitive
damages, or grievances.
No intentional lives ruined
from a tragic dysfunctional
family environment.
No bad deeds. No police mama to come to your house
to arrest your peace of mind, or rampage through your goods, or
wrestle your drawers, looking for contraband. That would
have caused such an outcry. No screaming or raised voices,
bickering back and forth, sounding like a new foreign language…
No racist to come with a big stick
to threaten your life. No leg cuffs,
to shackle you to a commitment

of a personal term, for an UN
determined number of years.
Only a death certificate
read: *Accident unknown, to be determined…* No alarms, no Billy
club, no matchstick, no lawyer screaming, "sit down… sign this,
take this plea." No frame. No bust. No dead body on the lawn
with a note, "Cancer took me too soon." No *Old Age Certificate.*
No level 6-felony offender. No Buddhist obstacle. No kid screaming
or sadly crying. No abrupt epiphany. No buzzword. No mice being
*defecated* on in their mazes, listening to Heavy Metal, trying to go back
home. No click, click, click, click, click, click, just dead.

# THE SLOTHFUL LANDLORD

I see her for the first time,
a conniving evil woman, hell bent on
ruining our vacation. A lying self-deprecating
*miniature Hitler*, carefully constructing


chaos: the dirt in the corners obviously untouched,
black hairs on the bathroom floor, embedded
in the rotting legs of the vanity, black beetles
casually crawling from behind the toilet, & in the living room,


dishes left cluttered in the dish drying rack, & still wet
when we first arrived, & the refrigerator bin was smeared
with mayonnaise. The previous tenant left bags of organic peas,
stacked in the freezer, & a myriad of strange, used condiments,


hung on the door. The internet service never connected, until three
magical days, before we had to go home. Dingy sheets were left
sloppily stacked on top of the beds, & the issue of the slight red
stain in the seam, of the middle couch pillow cover & barely visible,


& her insistence that we buy her a *brand-new* couch. The
teasing painting
of beach waves like white curling rope hung overhead the kitchen

doorway aiming to create a *normal* environment. Above the
fireplace, in the living room, a "Welcome to Paradise" sign hung
obtrusively.


One day, I noticed a trumpet flower vine, gracefully bobbing in the
window by the kitchen sink. The rain had spattered on it
in the evening, so it was lush & illustrious like an opera singer—
the only thing that remained viable, good & sweet, promising a
healing—a life


that would continue to erase the negativity of this landlord: her
poison entrails insisting we go home early, in her threatening
emails & voice messages.
The vodka bottle found chilling in the freezer, ready to explode,
still awaited.

# Dear Patient:

7/19/2016

We are hereby trying to collect payment for the following services:

Recommending you get a colonoscopy,
                    which removed a cancerous tumor.
                                        6/6/2002


Psychological services, to help you analyze a message,
from your now ex-best friend—
                    a former Air Force doctor, who told you to *go
back* to smoking, because your *flora*, was damaged and quitting
                    then, wasn't the right time.
                                        6/6/2003


Defaulting on making a payment to your now ex-wife after putting
a stop
                    on a $29,700 check, you gave to her, for
                    her share of money, from a check made out to *Mr.
                    and Mrs.*.... after she helped you win, a personal injury
                    lawsuit.
                                        6/6/2004


Using your ex-wife to bypass the lazy, New York City ER hospital
staff,
                    to call a New Jersey hospital, & impersonate a nurse

to get *your* medical records sent STAT, when you
were in cardiac arrest.

6/6/2009

Emergency Defibrillation and open-heart surgery from a Washington,
DC hospital, after you drove back home to New Jersey
from Florida with your girlfriend.

6/6/2013

Multiple stents to unblock years of cholesterol damage to your left
arterial

valve, which you complained, prevented you
from getting an erection.

6/6/2014

X-ray films, showing black chalky cardiac tissue—
the last photos of your life.

9/6/2014

And for the following requisite services:
Mending of your daughter's *broken heart*.

2/5/2004

3/27/2015

Sincerely,

Collections Department

# SEASIDE HEAVEN THE CONDO IN PARADISE AND TO DIE FOR

This is their haunt in the summer. Two older adults, one tall man, a
TV director by profession,
with white hair and glasses, who barely speaks a word, unless he
needs you to do something like
hold an elevator or something like that, and maybe he got drunk
one day, and he forgot
that he doesn't usually talk, and he said "hello." I just said "hi'
back politely. His eyes


are beady and he is nervous, and I don't know if maybe he's
showing a little dementia or not.
He doesn't appear to be constantly facetious, but underneath you
know he has this
mean, tight, rigid standard, and mode of operandi where
*business is business*. And I kind
of respect that he's in business and has that kind of professional-
ism about him. He and his wife


are kind of inseparable at times. But something tells me, he's pure
evil and so is his wife.
Madge has had tons of plastic surgery to the point where she
finally looks good. I remember
telling myself before this last surgery, *boy she really looks like
Frankenstein* and now
you can see her pretty light purple eyes, and there is still a smile
of evil, a glint alit in

the mouth again. But at one time they did let me borrow a ladder a few years ago,
when I was renovating my apartment, at the request of a bossy Au pair, who later had a nervous
breakdown, after having a panic attack. Summer is the busiest time for many of the residents
in the building, for they are all back from their winter hideaways and trying to get


reacquainted with their neighbors. This year they are renovating the building and squabbling
about how they want to go forward. The proposed renovations are more costly
than expected, and the whole time-consuming aspect of the plan bothers most. The disruption
of the buildings natural flow of exuberance will be challenged. Who wants to spend summer


dodging workmen and listening to trucks and carpenters hammering away? The bird's songs are annoying and dissonant, an interruption of the morning's meditation, where the universe is beckoning me to its window, to peer inside and see what I am missing, and trying to awaken me to a reality vaguely acknowledged on a regular day, but which breathes to me, now that I'm a


Chopra Meditation devotee, dedicated to harmonizing myself within the universe
for a relaxing eternity in absolute peace.

# If the world came to an end

I would miss coconut ice-cream bars, cold grapes, cherry fruit pops,
the morning waking like a lemon lightbulb over the Piermont marsh,
the sound of a woodpecker jabbing at the bark of trees in the summer,
the odor from cookouts, the orange sun rising every morning at 5:00 am.,


the smile of my wheelchair bound daughter Kyla with her dimples,
the pictures of exotic vacations & faraway islands, the rush and bob
of ocean water along sandy white beaches, seashells & coral reefs,
the healing minutes of soulful meditation, beautiful clothes, the number


118 on my scale, soft blue jeans, writing poetry & getting published,
posting on Facebook, Skyping, fudge brownies, fruit drinks, pizza,
ice water, dieting, reading magazines, Vaseline, dreaming pleasant
dreams & winning lottery tickets, going on vacation to Martha's
Vineyard,


acting out the characters in books for Kyla, playing games & listen-
ing to cool talking dolls, helping Kyla play the piano, strumming the
guitar, going to Broadway plays, doing rehab in San Diego,
Backstage magazine,
miracles—lots of fabulous unexpected miracles, driving my car,


the sky beaming like a watercolor painting, carousel rides,
little jewelry & clothing boutiques, the robin & blue jay both chirping

in the wee morning, the sun beaming in my bedroom window like a god sent starry angel, exploring Buddhism and Reiki, studying foreign languages,


wearing red nail polish, auditioning for movies, the color silver, the Bronx zoo, air popped popcorn, chocolate frozen low-fat yogurt, memories of Chock-Full O' Nuts hot dogs & Fit n Frosty shakes, the flight of planes in the clear blue sky, the NYC ballet, memories of standing room at the opera with Joseph,


traveling through my memory to Austria & the Czech Republic, riding the train, eating sherbet, ordering books from Amazon, writing screenplays, laughing, feeling happy, smiling, conjure parrots, Blow Pop lollipops, bubblegum, dark chocolate, vanilla soymilk, Starbucks coffee, green tea, TV, the winter Olympics, playing tennis, ice cubes, massages, swimming, falling in love & big, old yellow houses filled with family members and ghosts.

# INHERITING THE DINNERWARE

The same sour-ball green, glass dishes
& cups & saucers.
Godmother's green plates
& dishware all arrived one day.
Light gleamed through them
& maybe she didn't use them,
But I don't want anything to do with them.


This was it for me,
Because I don't want her bad luck
to rub off on me.
I avoid them—won't eat off of them
& they are too green.


Thinking about Ernie & his pots
& pans that my father inherited
& is cookingwith
& how I don't want to eat anything either
from those pots or pans that he had used.
I don't know them that well I think;
maybe I will die, if I eat off of theirplates.


Death arrives in little boxes;
tragedy arrives to live with us…
The ghost of each person gleaming in delight
& watching their deathlydishes

& pots & pans being used
as if they were occupying our lives
& it's like being at the funeral parlor with them
& my father's non-understanding
about my not wanting to use their belongings.


We inherited everything.
I refuse to eat off of them;
they come in a brown corrugated box
& the plates seem almost new,
stacked with the same pieces of brown paper
separating each green plate,
—from someone I had met only once,
but godmother had sent me a gift
every Christmas wrapped in thick brown paper
like the kind used to wrap meat
at the butcher shop or at the dry-cleaning store,
bundled with scotch tape
& my name written on the fat bundle
& a Santa Claus sticker in green with bells.


The yucky presents from death!
I have no idea If I will grow old—
Traveling along Kings Highway,
ducking under trees—in the woods,
guarding the way back home—even when it rains.
I feel lucky like I am in a rain forest.
Wild squirrels scramble up trees, possums
or scary rodents sneak into the woods
—& then I see roadkill with tails.

It is like one long path, always coming back,
after a trip from grandma's house.
Happy, I march a mile in the woods,
& dark green gleamed like evergreen.
The leaves hung like springs from the trees.


A yellow house sat on the left
& it was where the news finally hit me
that Ernie had died in a fire from smoking in his house.
He forgot to put his cigarette out.
I had visited his house once
& we had made a great big apple pie.


I think his house was a house in the woods
like that little yellow house—
Little Red Riding Hood's house
& him sleeping unable to get out.

The memory of death & the cold body,
like my pimply uncle who was so cold,
or my friend's father.
My grandmother Rhodes was the only one
who looked so beautiful, young & peaceful.

# ODE FOR GEORGE FLOYD

*"I have a dream." —Dr Martin Luther King Jr.*

Going to be somebody someday, no matter what the white man says.
Each and every day I pray, to never end up the way George was
slayed, obeying the law, non-resistant, polite, dressed nicely,
unarmed, and kind. Rights of African Americans have been
destroyed by a system of injustice, glorifying white supremacy,
inciting the knee to crush the breaths of humanity.

Each time I see a policeman use his power to end the life of a
person of color, fire burns in my eyes; lights get dimmed by the tears
flowing from my despise. Life is not about the white man, and his
arrogance using his stick and bullet to oppress the lives of so many
Americans, living their lives peacefully and free. Yesterday was only
a dream to so many, and we have so many more dreams to dream,

songs to sing, minds to bring the power to esteem! We
cannot waste lives being blind to the terror that police brutality
brings! Ignite the fire inside! Ignite the fire with all your pride.

Ignite the fire inside your mind. Be all that you can be. Power equals education! Very happy people go through tough times too, but they keep getting up again. Every time I see someone like George Floyd get abused, I literally want to cry, shout and scream "Au Secours, Au Secours!" I can't stand seeing a man in pain,


Then being demeaned and MURDERED because he is Black.
It upsets me! It upsets Nations across the world watching—
witnessing Police Brutality. It sends a  message
America is failing and deteriorating and disintegrating. Something must be done! Now and forever to change the course of our lives, so we can learn to love each other; learn to love each grandmother,


grandfather, father, brother, son, mother, sister, daughter like our own and respect them as our own. One life equals all our lives, equals all our futures, equals all our humanity, equals all our grandchildren. Now is the time to take no chances. Take no chances. Take no chances but stay alive!

# ODE TO THE BOTCHED SUICIDE ATTEMPT

There is something prophetic about a *Crazy ex-boyfriend*, driving
down the road, in his SUV and so angry, that you might be


a recovered sex-addict in a healthy relationship or maybe you *look*
like the *perfect victim,* he might want to land in heaven with


or at least nuzzle up to the pearly gates with, to beg for
forgiveness, where he'll cry and shout and dance around nude


saying "I haven't had any sex in years. My wife left me years ago
and ever since, I've been masturbating, but lately the batteries


in my cushiony, electric vibrator had a power glitch
and I got semi-electrocuted!"


Now he has got to wipe you out, before you do anything *fatal—*
something he wouldn't mind consider doing, like trying to hit


you head on, with your handicapped daughter in the back
seat, because *your life isn't important,* and neither is his

thinking how he would like to end it all, and use you, as a
catalyst, to ignite that rage bottled up inside, and now he's


ready to commit, half suicidal, after his wife slammed
the door in his face, after catching him boinking his neighbor's


wife, scrunched up in a too-tight Barbie doll-like dress,
painted on her shapely buttocks, the size of a


*oriental good luck lantern.* His brain was lit on fire with
the words "resurrect me baby!" spitting out of his larynx.


I looked that wild cat straight in the eye, and told him
with my Scorpio venomous eyes, *you better not you Sonofa!*


and he retreated like a dejected king cobra snake,
realizing his bite, wasn't powerful enough, to kill anybody,


not even his ashamed, cheating, self-loathing self.

# ODE FOR THE HUSBANDS WHOSE WIVES CARE LESS ABOUT THEM

I

Why do some women stop loving their husbands?
and let them eat themselves to death.
You can see they are not fit sex partners
with their bellies extended
like a Biafran child bloated from tapeworms,
and, dying of starvation.
It's just a horrible metaphor for spousal abuse.
But does it have to happen in America,
land of the free—
where food is not a scarcity but in excess?
What is the equalizer for hope or love?

II

If the weight is lost, it can be eradicated
and taken off the chaotic list
of *conditions non-eradicated.*
And I blame the wives of these men who are still
sexually hot and wanting of love
and ask them *why have they not been loved?*
If that were my man
I would give him Garcinia Cambogia
and be a constant guru
in buying him diet shakes, a bicycle,
and Weight Watchers classes.

III

I'd say to him "Gee honey,
here is the new menu;
isn't itdelicious?
And oh, can I make your lunch?"
Then I'd take it right out of the Weight Watchers box
and pretend it's made from scratch
and say "Oh, so delicious."

# ODE TO THE JEALOUS MOTHERS

Sunday is Mother's Day and all the mothers are waiting for something

great to happen to them, to win the lottery, or to receive some beautiful flowers,

fragrant flowers, flowers to die for, ones that everyone will be jealous of when

seeing their *name* on the gift card tacked on the plastic wrapping. For the husbands

who don't get it when their wives exclaim, "Oh, I wish those flowers were for me!"

"Are you sure, those aren't mine?" when passing through the lobby and there appears

a ravishing bouquet gleaming with petals that say, *eat your heart out,* twirling on the

concierge's counter. It's embarrassing not to get any presents from men, like on

Valentine's Day, when you're working in a hospital, and the sexy LPN gets a big basket

of flowers delivered to the floor, and cutely says, "They're from my husband," and you

can imagine she's married to this big jealous mobster, who prob-
ably guards every

step she takes, just by seeing her full body in her tight, white
polyester sprayed on

pants, and seeing her happily prepare the head nurse's *dead
mother* for the morgue.

The white linen sheet she meticulously puts over the old, withered,
arthritic body

now holy from cancer, the sun setting beautifully with orange kiss
rays, warming the

corpse through the windows. Is this the final denouement? —The
last chapter of life

draped with white sheets crisp and cool, and light heaving its
heavy heart before the

dead file into the morgue, slipped inside a sterile metal drawer, to
await the funeral

director, and ponder how gorgeous they will look, with lighter fluid
dripping over

them in their new dress that has been hanging in their closet for
centuries, for just

this day, when they get their first genuine makeover
to be remembered for eternity?

# ODE TO KINDNESS

Sometimes I just want to be kind,
when I'm putting my daughter back
on her 3-WHEELER bike
and she's pulling at my long hair, and
I'm thinking about how she's so
impulsive like I was as a child,
and I'm thinking about the autistic boy
I used to teach, who would need a time-out
when he had to go with a group of kids, to
play inside, and how he always wanted to be
first in line, and if he couldn't be first, he'd cry
and have a tantrum, and we'd have to let him
get angry, and I'm watching my daughter grow
and wondering how much of this
she has in her, and why it happens and maybe
it's better this way— she is expressing her wants
and needs, and this is the way she does it every day,
her way, the only way to get you to listen and see her
in all her fussiness and feistiness, to think about, what
she wants you to do,
to jump outside your comfort zone
and check the environment for comfortableness. But
I got it now. And did you not hear that?

# ODE TO MODEL WANNABES

Ever since you were young,
you've had this wild fantasy dream
to be a model.
You're 5'11 and 140 pounds.
You've been told that you're beautiful,
a million and one times, and now you're tired
of hearing it anymore. So, you've decided
to make it to New York City, and go to ELITE
modeling agency and be discovered.


You're not American, but you're European,
and you need a visa, so
you try to become an Au Pair
and get a job in New York City.
First thing you do when you get to NYC,
is you get your comp cards—
every model's calling card,
and you get dressed up
in your best glamour girl outfit.


You've even lost 10 pounds more,
even though you're already very skinny—
so skinny,
you can't even lift your 50-pound suitcase,
or climb a flight of stairs, without
huffing and puffing.
But you're sure now,
that you can make it into the agency.

You're there with your best *cover girl smile,*
and you're almost positive;
you've got it this time!
You have five minutes to impress them,
with your gaunt looks, your hollow cheeks,
your flat chest, your regurgitated food
growling in your stomach, and to beg them
to give you a golden life altering chance.


There is a line of a 1000, other girls
just as pretty, or as different,
waiting to be discovered.
Girls even skinner than you,
who tell you, they are too fat,
and they are 5'11 and 120 pounds,
and their legs are like pegs,
or ostrich legs, or pink flamingo legs,
and they wear pencil thin jeans.


When you tell them, they look like *death;*
they grimace with their capped teeth,
that cover the stains of acid reflux
and cigarette smoke, and bruxism
from too many dinners spent starving
and choking on the stars
that seem to glitter every night the same way,
even when they're dying,
to stay thin, thinner, thinnest, thinned,
just almost.

# ODE TO MY CONTACT LENSES

Oh, the joy of Contact Lenses!
They can cause the diseases of the eye most surely
to get you angry. The plastic inserts
like little, pea-size pills, you pop in the morning.
Oh, the frustration of cleaning them with saline
without ripping them or inserting them too fast,


and they are inside out, and rough like a little zipper covering
your cornea or feel like a small spike is in your eye. But I still
wear them, in spite of despising them
late into the evening, after my eyes are threadbare like rags
and heavily exhausted, hung like little bouncy springs.
Oh, the joy of the morning,


When I remember to take them out—
wondering first if they are really in,
when I feel an impediment like a rock
and I'm trying to wipe away my cornea—
thinking it's a contact, and if it is the contact,
I can't seem to grasp it, and slide it off my eye


back into the warm solution, jiggling in its case.
These lenses are better than getting laser surgery
to make your eyes 20/20—
where you could possibly go blind, if the laser fails.
Sometimes it feels like coke bottles—
are crushed down inside my eye's anterior chamber,

mixing with the aqueous fluid,
because the lens is folded in half, aching
like a glass dagger,
and torn like a paper doily flitting around.
How I long for the contact lens, thin like air
which can magically massage the gentle eye


back to 20/20 vision over time—
A real cure for the blind and severely frustrated.

# ODE TO BREASTFEEDING

My mother had perfect nipples:
Thick, plump, brown, wedge cap eraser size nipples.
She was the envy of every failed mother
Who couldn't get her child, to latch-
On or who couldn't get her milk
To flow. Those ideal perfect spouts
For sucking in warmth and nutrition—
Immunity from death
And disease in the early childhood
Years. How I tried to imagine my incompetent nipples
Were pert and primped; I squeezed and stroked
Them to make them radiate like love itself—
To pour my sweet sustenance into
My baby's mouth, as my arms rocked and snuggled
My baby Kyla. I wasn't a total failure—but how
I wanted the non-collapsible, super-duper nipple
That never got tired!

# ODE TO TAKING VITAMINS

Oh, the vitamins we take that help keep us skinny.

To the ones that help the brain mend damaged brain cells.

To the ones that help the cholesterol exit the body.

To the ones that help ease the nerves.

To the ones that improve cognitive function & memory.

To the ones that make us feel smarter & more acute.

To the ones that taste good & are orange & sweet—

We gobble them like candy.

To the ones that help prevent the cold & the flu.

To the ones that help keep bones strong & our moods elevated.

To the ones that make us say *I love my body & soul.*

To the ones that give us razzamatazz!

# ODE TO DARK CHOCOLATE

You make my brain eutrophic—
Just one square, I know you care
Tenderly & I kiss
Your brown lips, until
I can't have you anymore.


You can smooth me, groove
Me, lovely daughter, Kyla,
Like a dark chocolate,
And you're the only one—
Who is warm as summer sun


Crooning, win, win, win; you say
Open vowel & throat vibrating
Like a trilling bird, welcoming
Reeds & rain & sugar cane.
And oh, how I love you.

# ODE TO RETURNING TO THIS LIFE

*for my sister*

What's the purpose of living?
We're here—
What are we to do with our lives?


Our belly buttons are nicely shaped—
Clean not dirty—no crust.
We were born nicely—


No C section for mom. We cried
When we wanted. Bottle fed—
We pulled to stand on time,


And walked on time.
Where was the conflict?
We caused no chaos, except


When I almost died at two-years-old.
Playing and crawling then I stopped breathing.
Did I forget to breathe or was it a heart problem?


Then our parents shook me frantically and I was back.
Had I gone to the other side for a while? —
Pondered about, saw God and spoke to him,

Held his hand, made peace with him…
Why had I come back? Was it the warm,
Prodding fingers of mom and dad? —


Their good looks and my feeling sorry for them—
A handsome couple, they loved their baby.
And if you really want an answer why—
To not have you be lonely anymore.

# ODE TO SAMMY DAVIS Jr.

Sammy was a man with a smile
that could knock down any barrier.
He owned a golden voice,
so smooth & pleasing
even to the hearty warrior.
His voice was a remedy
for your everyday woes.
He had a voice of a lover,
not a loner. You could hear him
daily, & never tire of his valor!


Sammy, your songs grooved
the nerves—so smooth
like a sweet, sultry flower.
You made life a dreamy scene.
Whenever I hear you,
I feel such joy!
You sang songs like a modern god
—-you were the best, &
your rhythm weaned
fatigue from my bones,
all lovely night long.


Life is a ride, singing with you
& I am high in the sky.
Come sail away with me!
Can't you see,

how wonderful life can be?
All my dreams can turn
into a reality!
We can laugh & sing forever.

# ODE TO THE BEVERLY HILLS DIET

The diet phenomenon where you will never go hungry again!
Welcome, to Judy Mazel's adventure, where all your food fantasies


Become a reality! Never again will your emotions take
Control over your life. Eating does not have to make


You miserable. No more deprivation, sleepless nights,
Laxatives, diuretics, or feeling ashamed to step on your


Scale. Now eating will bring you energy and optimism.
You can eat like a *mensch* knowing you can have anything


If you plan for it! Food equates to all your best memories
Of happiness, love, office parties, romance, winning at


Lotto, Tennis tournaments and you don't have to feel
Deprived since there are no limits on how much you can eat


But when you eat. Conscious combining is everything!
If you understand food, that it is not just a taste in your mouth,


But it can work for you and not against you. You will learn
To, make food your best friend, not your best enemy.

Food is your first love; the antidote to your depression,
Loneliness, heart break, jealousy, sadness, and boredom.


But on the Beverly Hills Diet all that will end! No more
Going to bed feeling fat, and like a failure; no more hours


Spent on a treadmill. No more self-hate when waking up and
Being afraid to jump on the scale. No more blowing it,


And worrying what new diet to start in the morning.
No more prescriptions for failure. No more thinking


About dieting and thinking suffering, self-abuse, punishment.
No more hungry memories, where you felt deprived. No


More feeling controlled by what you love: FOOD. You will
Be able to eat what you love without feeling guilty and ashamed,


As long as you plan for it. You're getting better and being fat
Will be a thing of the past, a worn-out belief that you can't


Indulge in fattening foods. The all-consuming-diet-consciousness
Will have been blotted out forever from your mind! Your support


System will be installed by wearing the Golden Pineapple
Emblazoned on your chest— testament to your eternal slimness!

# ODE TO THE BREAK-UP

Oh, I *PROCRASTINATE* (wow procrastinate, is a powerful
Endnote)—


The throbbing numbness,
Gross end result that comes from this realization


Must mean finality.
—The *end* has come!


I go there, to that
Balcony/cliff where the word is perched


Like Larry Flynt's exclusive sex club "HUSTLER"
Wildly glittering in neon red lights, in the wicked wind.


I want this to end—
This relationship!


I need to know that
Hanging            out           by           this
Abyss, where the word *procrastination* hangs solemnly,

I'll survive, if you breathe life gently back
Inside the little forgotten me.


I need to let this voyage send me
To this crawlspace, occupy my pain—


Wrap it like a fresh cut of beef; clean it like a dirty diaper;
Hook it like a white whale; brush the hardened


Bristle from the bud of pain;
Simmer then shake,


The burnout;
Free the aches of indecision, away from the heart,


Smooth joy into them, and then let them ride home free!

# ODE TO SELF PRESERVATION

I remember the time in 4rd grade,
the little brother of Joey called me a *Nigger*


and I was just waiting in line to catch the school bus
to go home, standing in the cafeteria, where Woody,


the custodian would shout "Don't forget your lunches!"
so vividly that I remembered his voice playing in my head


a couple of years ago, when I was taking a hot bath
in my Jacuzzi, and feeling like he was a part of me


as intrinsic like bark is to a tree. I don't remember
the "N" word penetrating my skin and making a cut.


It didn't sully my pretty complexion or take the sun out
of the red in my hair or take the joy out of my heart.


The room didn't spin or get me dizzy. I just saw hate
spewing it's ugliness like a hornet's nest had been sprung

loose from its hiding place, fallen from a treetop
and cast like a demon from hell. That little boy


would remain in my mind, a miniature minitour—
deformed and beastly, like the animal he had behaved like


on that day, so long ago, when the sun shone down
from heaven, into the garden, outside our bus line


in that cafeteria, with the stage curtains of
faraway planets whirling in my memory.

# ODE TO INNOCENCE

One, hot, summer day, when I was vacationing
With, my family, at the Hudson Guild Farm,
home Alone, in the cottage, I dug my
tablespoon inside the ice-cream container, and
ate from it,

Over the kitchen sink, after being caught,
On the Verge of making love, to my little Black boyfriend.
He had knocked on my door and called for me to come
Outside, around where the grass was flaxen and tall,

And I most surely did as I was told, and I
Remember seeing his little black penis, and
Half of his bare behind, and me standing in
Grass and him unabashed, irrelevant of

Anyone around. I know we didn't
Enjoy *coitus*, and settle into any
Enjoyment, before a white woman, who was hanging
Her whitewash, then turned around saw/caught me

By the eye, scowled and chased us apart, and so
I retreated back, inside the cottage. I remember
Feeling coolly unashamed about what happened
Relishing in *Borden's* vanilla bean, chocolate
And, real strawberry ice-cream with little sticky
Hands owning the cardboard carton,

And my chestnut brown bangs tousled over my right
Eye, as I stood, on a tall chair, over the kitchen sink

Looking out through the window, with sun
Shining in on me, like a *Paradisiac Star,* and
Getting on with the business of being five,
And thanking God, *my mother didn't catch me!*

I wonder what became of him.
Did he *Remember* us, and our failed attempt?
Was he now proficient, in the ways of *wooing,*
One's lover into the bed? Did he have any

*Misgivings*, about what could have been, at that small

Age, when our plastic brains were rapidly being
Instilled, with vivid memories? I ask myself—
Can one *forget*…he or I, that desire to lie

Resplendent, on a summer day? And how sacred
Our innocence was gently sweetened.

# ODE TO THE SUPER DELIVERY MAN

After Dulce Pinzón, *Superman.*


Superman travels to Brooklyn
every day on his blue bike
delivering pizza to the hood
homies/mommies/junkies/workers.


He's from the state of Pueblo
& sends $500.00 a week
home to his family.
"They love me," he says, esteem


beaming from his dark, olive size eyes.
His red cape is flowing in the din
& his chiseled, black-haircut, is razor-
like from the wind blowing smog wildly.


His tiny, thin black mustache hides
a small smile expressing
"Gee I'm making it; I'd never survive
without this *Job* back home."


Pride & joy beam across his chest
emblazoned with a Big red "S"

over his light blue & white costume.
The one made just for him, the hero—


The man refusing to take pity.
The man refusing to die poor.
The man refusing to commit suicide.
The man refusing to run and hide.

# ODE TO BUYING A CEMETERY PLOT

Oh, the task of picking out the plot of land to finally rest in.
The spot by the bubbling stream.
Oh, how marvelous to hear the water rush by,
After the rain, on a summer sunny day.
Awakening the memory of the rusty red-haired dogs, running
Around, wagging their tails, when I was but a wild, wee child.
And riding my ten-speed bike around and around the circle there
And, singing to the gravestones
—My audience! — loving those poets whose poems
Shone on their stones.


Oh, how I yearned to be a movie star
& singer like Barbara Streisand! But this was not to be
—A songwriter perhaps, or a poet. Both careers later called out to
me.


Oh, shall I find a resting place at the top near the Pathfinder
Overlooking the Hudson river,
Or near the newer plots of land sloping down a hill?


What bed of roses, shall I lay my weary body down onto?
What perfumed earth shall hug my old, tattered soul?
What entry to the other world will I buy a key for?

# ODE TO GRATITUDE

Alchemist turn darkness into light—
Sourceness of all the hinges in life.
We live, and we realize
Our own level of perfection—
The ability to breathe
The experience of our senses:
Miracles that happen over and over
Touch the leaves on the trees.
Thank the earth for the abundance
That it provides—
See the miracles as they ripple outward
Touching the hearts of all humanity.
Gratitude is my prayer— gratitude is my power…

# ODE TO HEARTBURN

I knew this woman who complained;
she thought she was going to have a heart attack.
I couldn't believe it! She wanted to go to the emergency room.
She was very skinny and exercised daily.

I didn't know what was going on.
She was crying with her hands covering her face, and
she said she had a dream,
and in it her mother told her to *go home*.

Her mother was dead and had died from injuries
she sustained, after she had been beaten
when some men came into her refugee camp.
She saved her child, but was wounded and

eventually died from complications.
Her father had been assassinated by poisoning;
he was a general in the Namibian Army,
who one day broke from his usual routine with his bodyguard.

I never thought you could die from a broken heart.
But her boyfriend had also left her for her best friend.
Those chest pains were most likely heartburn
like the pains I'm feeling now.

As I look back through the pile of my failed relationships,
I feel better just writing about them.

# ACKNOWLEDGEMENTS:

I want to thank my father Joel Rhodes who suggested I write some funny poems and my mother Rosemarie Rhodes and sister Leslie Ann Rhodes for their support to write poetry.

Grateful thanks to Gigi Silverman, Christopher Citro, Alexander Weinstein, Aubrey Crosby, Martha's Vineyard Institute of Creative Writing community, Claudine Nash, Dan Masterson, Jeffrey McDaniel, Suzanne Cleary, Michael Affa Weaver, Francine J Harris, Cornelius Eady, Nicole Sealey, Jacqueline Jones Lamon, Monica Youn, Donald Fisher, Kevin Pilkington, Greg Roman, Michael Collins, Myronn Hardy, Jean Valentine, Billy Collins, Susan Guma, Thomas Lux, Sarah Lawrence College & Alumni, Ross Gay, Poets Corner, Douglas Brown, Evie Shockley, Joan Silber, Martha Rhodes, Erika Meitner, Adam Levon Brown, Dustin Pickering, Shittu Fowora, Mariana Goicoetxea, Joan Larkin, Gregory Pardlo, Cave Canem, River River Writers Circle, Rockland Poets where some of these poems were first heard and numerous others.

Thanks to the following publications where these poems or earlier versions first appeared:

*Talking Writing:* Why I Shouldn't Worry So Much

*SLOTH 7 Deadly Sins Vol. 4:* The Slothful Landlord

*The Writers Café Magazine:* Dear Patient; Ode to the Husbands Whose Wives Care Less About Them; Rendezvous at the Azalea Garden Restaurant; Peripeteia; Inheriting the Dinnerware

*Dash Literary Review*: Ode to the Jealous Woman

A sincere thanks to Dr. Karunesh Kamur Agarwal, managing editor of Taj Mahal Literary Review for helping bring these poems to a larger audience.

* 9 7 8 9 3 8 8 3 1 9 3 1 7 *